MW01015934

The rainforests hold answers
to questions we have yet to ask.

~ *Mark Plotkin*

1

Rainforest
in
Russet

by
Cynthia Sharp

Silver Bow
Publishing

Box 5 – 720 – 6th St.,
New Westminster, BC
V3C 3C5 CANADA

Rainforest in Russet
Author – Cynthia Sharp
Copyright © 2018 Silver Bow Publishing
Cover Design: Candice James
Layout/Design: Candice James

ISBN 978-1-927616-80-2 (print softcover)
ISBN 978-1-927616-81-9 (electronic book)

Library and Archives Canada Cataloguing in Publication

Sharp, Cynthia (Poet), author
     Rainforest in russet / by Cynthia Sharp.

Includes index.
Poems.
Issued in print and electronic formats.
ISBN 978-1-927616-80-2 (softcover).--ISBN 978-1-927616-81-9 (PDF)

     I. Title.

PS8637.H3762R35 2018   C811'.6   C2018-903971-X
                                              C2018-903972-8

Silver Bow Publishing
Box 5 - 720 Sixth St.,
New Westminster, BC
CANADA V3L 3C5

Email: info@silverbowpublishing.com
Website: www.silverbowpublishing.com

Rainforest in Russet

Dedicated

To everyone who supported my writing journey from way back in my York creative writing days to my current communities in Pandora's Collective, The Royal City Literary Arts Society and Writers International Network, with much gratitude to Ken Ader, Jacqueline Carmichael, Coranne Creswell, Candice James, Ken Johns, Fiona Tinwei Lam, Jude Neale, Emily Olsen and everyone at Silver Bow Publishing and the Simon Fraser University Writer's Studio.

Acknowlegements

Thank you, Jude Neale, for your huge heart and collaboration with me on the title poem of this book *"Rainforest in Russet";* and I also thank *Antarctica Journal, Ascent Aspirations Magazine Friday's Poems, CV2, Lantern Magazine, The Piker Press, Prolific Press, Street Light Press, Toasted Cheese* & *untethered* for earlier publications of several of these poems.

Table of Contents

The forest doctors of the Amazon say
each plant has its "song",
and to know how to use the plant
you must listen to its voice.

~ Jay Griffiths

Rainforest in Russet

In the silence
between
breaths,

my truth rises.

I fall into the space
where the forest

captures
light.

Is this the question
or the answer?

To trust this journey of closure?

A new opening repertoire -
I dig for you

in the shadows of dying
grey matter,

to find a slip,

a morsel
of foggy memory.

How we set up your chessboard
the night we met.

Photographed the pieces

in their complicity
to be seen as art.

The queens,

their own fashion statements
balanced in the spotlight.

The horses rode across
the checkered landscape,

free of battle
scars or fear.

Configurations
came and went.

We both knew the game
transcended competition,

our strategy
a decades long
tango of connection.

We played until
slivers of dawn

shone

onto an empty stage.

Now at the threshold
of rainforest in russet,

ash into earth,
to whatever is or isn't,

I am released.

Perseid Showers

leaf lanterns glow under stars
dried flowers line
an evergreen cathedral
rainforest lit up
we lie on the cool earth
our own mythology

Bliss

moonlit
cherry petals
under fireflies and stars
the love I still believe will come
risen

The Sojourner's Way

in the haven of silence
I no longer carry
everyone's blind spots
put some of it down
let nirvana return

fallen tree uprooted no more
thunder, rain, time
cherry petals in a sea of blue
the swoosh of a sand stream
emptied of unwanted current
gentle mist beyond

slow journeys
the softness of wind in birch leaves
heart of green   earth   breathing
these afternoons before I go to forest

only a tiny fraction makes it to the light
but that fraction embodies all

For All the Flowers

There is nowhere I need to be,
only the desire
to stand out in the sun.

How to Honour the Moon

Like the fragrant colours of May
descending like manna
from citrus-tinted branches
of blossoms in the rain,

like the silence of the days,
a flow of unspoken story
moving softly through
an abundance of petals,

like current dreams
travelling light,
an orchid that slowly
courageously opens,

she is always near,
blessing our sanctuary,
no matter how far we travel
from the rhythms of home –

be gentle with her spirit
allow for her light,
every broken moment
made whole in her divinity.

Call of the Light

Cherry petals in early sun
from grey branches
smooth as desert bones
allow the quiet
vibrations of self
to surface –
the sanctity of spring,
a holy ground
for one's own voice.

Cycles

Leaves deepen richly,
three-quarter moon
preparing for birth.

Gratitude

The shades of orange
in the petals of a daisy,
the scent of sea in summer,
the beach on a Tuesday evening,
sunlight and slower days,
the way it's possible
to love again,
a groundedness in home,
like the stars there every night,
waiting on the moon.

Simplicity

droplets of water
glisten on misted needles
breathing the blue night

dawn awakens blooms
canopy rustles with wind
butterflies alight

clothes drying in sun
dragonfly comes to visit
momentum of grace

Dreaming with Tulips

From a bulb inside earth's womb
roots penetrate the soil.
Luminous through snow
candescent colours
overflow the boundaries of time.

Aspiring to be sunflowers
in September wind,
tulips vibrantly answer the call –
stems grow beyond
ocean-washed glass from the shore
along the edges of vases,
curve like rivers,
forge in new directions
and define for themselves
who they are.

Unafraid of transition,
tulips allow the flow of life
to turn their insides
into buttercup yellow elixir
falling on fairies
like a gentle halo –
Ophelia's spirit
risen.

A Tribute to Orange

the changing leaves
in the cherry tree by my balcony
welcoming cooler mornings
of coffee and cream,
the moon in harvest time,
tea and tiny cakes,
my first Mid-Autumn Festival
in an apartment in Burnaby
as I tutored students in poetry,
the generosity of the girls
serving me with two open palms
and sending me home with extra

the colour of the tie-dyed skirt
I admired in the window
of a high-end Granville shop
forty-five dollars I didn't have
that whole summer
years later I returned
and purchased an orange top at Roots
that I wear with the memory
of the window skirt
from the summer of '97
when I had been sleeping
on two separating couch cushions
in a smoky basement
amazed at the possibility
of a new life in BC,
the first time I saw
a four-dollar coffee
spending all of
what I had left of my savings
on beverages at Starbucks
for the family that housed me
in their basement

the light of the sun
as I purchased my first book in BC
Timothy Findley's *Memory*
at a second-hand bookstore on Granville
eight dollars a shock –
eight times more than what we charged
at the Book Market in my old hood
and totally worth every last dollar

the hue of fall
when I returned to BC for work
and the moon I fell in love under
in my thirties off Commercial Drive,
my Wiccan boyfriend
singing tunes to the spirits
through all-nighters and essays
student teaching
and me falling in love
despite the fact he was leaving

the embers in a film
I saw in kindergarten,
how they held me in meditation
the first time I lost myself
into a moving image
like I had with the orange and yellow angel
in the Advent calendar
I stared at her so long
seeking my spirit self
the shaman within

the colours of the healing chakra light
in my raven dream
sparks of yellow and orange
as children danced
safely in a circle
and my spirit protected them
my calling to become raven
he didn't miss the colours at all
he is all of them

the pencil I chose for the triangles
in my grade eight math book
the notebook I sat up
in the early morning
redoing in bed
in fear it was not neat enough
the first time
the light orange shade calming
my anxiety and post traumatic stress disorder

the piece of cloth
we got for two dollars in Montreal
covered in stars
and the candle I got to match
how I imagined it
as the floor of the mud hut
in my first novel of street life
before it travelled with me into videos
of loss and healing and finally
the student productions of
Shakespeare's *Midsummer Night's Dream*

the colour of the first image
I imagined in French
when I was tutoring a beloved student
who could read my mind

the shiny hue I chose
for my first pedicure
and admired all summer
barefoot at English Bay
soft sand between white toes
and a rhinestone that I valued
like a diamond

October in Elgin Street Park
where my grandparents met
the roses my Australian friend painted
when I presented them to her
a hostess gift for the home cooked dinner
preceding her children's evening recital

my favourite Cotton Ginny shirt
my grandparents bought me in Florida
the day we sampled fresh-squeezed juice
in tiny cups from the back of the truck
my grandma's adoration even richer
than all the light of Miami

the cover of my beloved
Alice Walker poetry book
painted like the walls
of my Thirteenth Avenue apartment

the glow of the neighbor's porch light
through rain
amber warmth reflected in puddles
like Paris café candles in the night

the first colour I see
mixed with violet
when I close my eyes

dancing with thunder

melodic leaves swirl
spiral embraced
dynamic partner

Shipwreck

prime light
first sun on skin
bodacious, eternal
before stingy controllers marred
our path

After the Fire

sea air
breathing again
a floating Wordsworth cloud
still aching for my own real life
blue sky

the dreaming after the storm

I look for the shaman,
a trickster of disappearing,
remembering how I too
saw auras and colours,
peace emerging through
mystical trances,
a healing touch of grace
as stories passed through me,
and I wonder if she is inside me.

Solstice Blessings

A splatter of droplets
on the last ruby leaf
of the Japanese maple,
a flutter of tangerine twirls
through misted stillness
above the blue mountain –

meditative calm
of winter womb time,
solstice moon
a swirl of creation,
like clouds of butterflies
swaying in a cradle,
the elegance of the flow
a call to sanctity within,
like Gaia bringing light
out of darkness,
as a flower holds the sun –

like a babe against
its Mamma's breast,
we are children in the night,
pausing with the empty trees
to take it all in,
breathing the beauty
of right here.

Crescent Moon

Tranquil branches rest
under a pastel sky,
waves slow to a heartbeat,
rhythms of winter
subsiding to spring,
like light from an ended star.

The seashore blessed
in caramel and lilac shells,
like Aurora Borealis
sprinkled across the sand,
brave bare soles and paws
taste the cool ripples,
the strength of kindness
in every changing season.

Baptism

Bowing before Jericho Beach,
twilit in rose,
I dip delicately into
the saline womb of the sea,
let the ocean water
flow through my fingertips,
pan across the Pacific horizon
to the harbour,
where the calls of gulls
override the garrulous city behind.

Salient pearl-capped waves
entice the shore,
wend along the winding coast,
coalesce in memory,
abrade the jagged rocks
of my soul,
wash over me
as I await entrance –

Transcendent touch of grace
trickling across
the mosaic of broken shells
like a wind chime
sifts the remains,
gently letting go
of all I never needed.

Take Flight

Take flight
from inside the cathedral,
as red roses bloom into the
ataraxia of summer days,
the fragrance of perfumed peonies and rain
the wind brings in the window
a calling to trust
this place in the universe and time,
a humbling beauty
akin to the rich harmony
of bows traversing the strings
of violins in worship.
Like Mary Magdalene hand washing clothes,
her palms cold and pink
in the sanctity of starlit cypress in the night,
let the deep purple jacaranda and
earth through our feet
align through the steeple
to the temple and tempo
of this sacred present moment.

Into the Heart

Cracked from the core,
the wounded self surrenders
to the healing turquoise
love of the universe.
To break is to let the light in and out,
where it is renewed
in the source of all,
to give beyond what kindness
we thought possible,
like winter trees
reaching across the stillness,
the fractured pieces of ourselves
truly more beautiful
for their wisdom in the flow of life.
When sun shines on shattered clay,
when water smoothes its edges,
we hold our brokenness
in our open palms,
trusting the privilege to serve.
In brokenness we release
the construction of perfect images,
to be made whole
in love,
in our humanity,
in service,
spirit rising like a phoenix.

sunfish in the sky
clouds dipping like quick minnows
turning lavender

Poppies and Dragonflies

poppies and dragonflies
in the grace of the wind
ancestral spirits call

Inventory

In the quiet of the students
having gone,
I leave the lights off,
invite my soles to rest
along the cream and tan patterns
of soft wool carpet,
take in the changes –
deeper crescents and stars
in my palms –
embrace a slower pace –
the swirl of clouds and
sway of elegant branches
in the summer night –
walk in the rustling of wind
through green leaves,
sit down at the coffee shop,
admiring the espresso art
in the cappuccino foam,
absorbing the calm of fading flowers
elegantly relaxing over the edge of a white vase,
as new buds blossom above.
I inhale the scent
of lingering perfume
through the tender petals of pink roses,
no longer having to run
to a next appointment
and reflect
on the honour it was
to commune
with each one of them.

amid quiet full trees

waking up in June with sunlight and time
the invisible rise up
the way the tips of the dogwood touch clouds
and luminosity returns
waiting on the birth

demi-moonlit night
September cool in the air
deep in love with you

Last days of summer,
our lips tingle with citrus,
your ghost vanishes
as the moon aches for the night,
circling the Earth to come back.

A Mid-Autumn Night's Dream

The night shimmers in elixir,
golden maple leaves soaring
like billowing sails
whose story is the mystical sea,
fairy queen beds and pillows
cascading like spring blossoms,
Titania's fall cocoon
of colour and quiet –
and even if the sky
lets down too much rain,
isn't it enough
to enjoy the radiance
of now?

Autumn's Kintsugi

The autumn palette amid Robson shops
a callback to the bustle of
Greenwich Village in student days,
he brings me an almond latte
beneath the heat lamps,
then we walk through Stanley Park cedar,
belonging to one another,
sounds of coffee and summer fading
into the rose line of fall sunset.
Above Third Beach in cool wind,
southbound geese travel the sky,
nature as always –
the birch and maple
at peace on the mountain,
leaves fluttering like
petals of gold in the wind,
the natural erosion of passion into love,
cream and caramel butterflies
finding their way
into the light of the world.

Remembrance

When you look at your palms,
what stories do they hold?
What spirits have you loved?
What work have you done?
What have your hands built?
What children have they held?
Have they washed dishes,
served coffee, poured tea?
Painted pictures, cleaned the containers,
wiped the room down?
Have they soothingly filtered sand or
tenderly touched the smooth
ocean-washed stones by the sea?
What strength is in your fingertips?
Do they lightly brush
the hair from a child's eyes?
Press deeply into the strings of a guitar?
Gently caress your partner's skin?
What stories are in your hands?

To All the Twitter Poets

your words solid and quiet
gliding in moonlight
the sound of warm water
seeping into earl grey leaves
140 characters of soul
little breaths of time
hearts speaking freely
in the sanctity of night
a bridge to souls
who love deeply and true
you are the place I come
to be understood

Silent Grey

snowed in with poetry
an open window
on the night sky

dances with trees
the movement of verse
through my heartbeat

beyond

i want to fall
into something deeper

your body
a poem

The Summer We Never Had

In the summer we never had,
there is time,
for endless evenings
of coffee and poetry
amid the spark of fireflies
in the city heat.

As voices from late night
gatherings on porches
drift in open windows,
I no longer pretend
you are in my room
just to study.

We are no longer pending
on outside approval,
only the potential
we elevate
in each other.

In the summer we never had,
I don't have to be
anything more than I am
and it doesn't matter
that my hair finds its way
into dreadlocks.

There is red wine and passion,
daisies that last the night –
my single bed is luxurious enough
and I never have to get over you.

I taste forever
how it would have been
and never let you go.

The Bohemian

A tribute to a favourite haven, the Café Bohemian,
and the guy who captured my heart so many years ago

I remember
spring brunches on the crowded patio
with high-school mates
in ripped denim jeans,
how we would cram into benches,
too many to a seat,
discussing guitar players
beneath the Rideau bridge
over pancakes
and coffee with cream –

my first waitressing job,
donning my name tag
with nervous enthusiasm,
prepping the tables
with fresh linen and carnations,
then opening the doors
to the lunch time rush –
transfixed in the chemistry,
our first connection,
my future unlocked,
versions of the days' events
an energy of stories
we would create for each other –

the electricity of our lunch dates
and all of our twenties,
gazpacho soup and grilled cheese
the summer standby,
endless caffeine
and engaging connection.
I remember
trading heels and trays
for a putative prospect in publishing
and you disappearing

along the way,
as I lost myself
into late autumn evenings,
a lonely barge along the night river,
still seeking you
as red leaves fell softly
into dark water.

There were winters
of penne Alfredo and anecdotes
catching up with university friends,
awkward exes, work acquaintances and
Saturday nights of long conversation.

I remember your return,
a wolf drawn to the moon
knowing I would resonate
with the timbres of your silent call

but mostly I remember
it was the last place I saw you.

Somnambulant Web

To the love I was abducted from,
a satellite to my being,
the raven trickster who elevates everyone
to laughter from deep within,
soaking in the sun that surrounds you –

Time lapses in your absence –
a stencil of easier days
like cut-out paper dolls without heart
mirrors vainly what used to be,
before I was taken

        I seek crosses in bamboo reflections,
        as a two-dimensional world
        plays fresco patterns across the stucco –
        ancient hieroglyphics move up and down
        in the shadows,
        weaving a language I can't decipher.

I dream I faked death to reunite with you,
lost in appliances and clothes at unwanted retail jobs,
the stillness of afternoons when you're gone.

        Reborn, a moment,
        my hope sprinkled with pyrite,
        the twins I wanted to have
        press their palms into my uterine wall,
        cave art from inside the womb.

Meteors of moonlight flicker across paintings,
fool's gold dissolving through my fingers –
I want there to be an excuse, a reason,
but there's not.

        I hold on
        because deep down,
        I know,
        there was only you.

You fell through crevices,
disappeared into another life
you make work,
and I am left clinging
to fragments.

Selenophilia

Reflecting back
to long lost loves and youth,
days of working in restaurants
in fast-paced east coast cities
and falling in love
under stars and fireflies at night,
I surrender my sorrow
to the cherry petals,
fluttering on the wind
like a thousand tiny butterflies
lingering in the light

Between Now and Yesterday

There is no tide that releases the hold
our connection had on my being.
The moon fills slowly in the winter sky,
our hearts still beating
in places we've left behind.

I walk in the green
and relax at the shore,
but the loss of us
still catches in my throat
like the absence of fireflies.

Respite

Night is for heartbeats
across ponds of frozen moonlight,
when the world is still
and the ache of how right we were
is all that resounds –

when silent spirits
hear my vibrations
through quiescent frost,
resurrect me
to the flow of true self,
I absorb you from disappearing
and we fly,
whole and separate beings,
before the weight of the snow
cracks branches in daytime.

Remainder 1

No matter how real it was,
waiting never brought you home.
But what is home?
You moved on
right where you were
and I, abducted away,
held to a specter
of what we deserved to be.

Chemical Collision

They tell me that he married –
I dream about him,
a wizard on a bridge
juggling just one ball,
looking back at me
the way the body remembers.

Amaranthine

When all my beauty is gone
and I'm an old hermit poet,
last wisps of hair
letting go to the wind,
I'll still be dreaming
of the life
we would have had,
feeling you
on the mountaintop
with me,
ever my one
even if I didn't
get to be yours.

Falling Stars

In the starlight of your ashes,
a newly blossoming plumeria flower,
how you would lie beside me
and when I gently awoke
tell me what I had said in my sleep,
a communion of adoration that continues
beyond your earth walk –
rose petals at midnight
shape the moonlight,
passionate and infinite
strength of tender beauty.

The Emerald

Scattered amid plumeria and orchids,
dandelions, once a pesky weed,
the barnacle of the garden,
now animate the earth,
velvet summer adjacent
to aged rosewoods bearded in moss,
the fragrant scent of pollen
transformed into wine and salad greens.
I cast a thousand wishes through the winds of time,
my fortune of seeds dispersed across the forest floor –
the emerald returns
to prune through tufts of feathery florets
and build its nest in soft dandelion and honeysuckle.
In the fervent flash of hummingbirds you rise,
spirit aflutter in their wings.
I turn your ashes anew –
you are here,
salt from the sea washed ashore.

Pine Boughs and Sweetgrass

Pine boughs curve gently into the sky,
spiraling through clouds.
Beneath their frosted amber,
tiny pearls on slender teal twigs
hold steady as wind
moves through gossamer.

From crow's vermillion throat,
a call through all the shades of grass.
The sun speaks patterns of flight
on textured elm trunks.
Everything eventually
holds part of the story.

Bowing below tangerine, lemon and lime,
ivy leaves turn crimson,
voices of endurance locked deep inside.
Mica dissolves to dust,
the richness of my grandfather's soul
ascending in the charcoal sky.

Savoury scents of summer
woven into prayer
by the warmth of the oven –
kettle whistles like
a chinook across the plains,
sweetgrass in the wind.

A Winter Tapestry

In silvered cedar lies the hope
the garden gives to all,
inviting realm of peace
in the depths of winter soil.
The tears and memories and hands
of all that went before
listen for movement in stillness,
Earthen darkness spun to ochre
like consciousness birthed into light.

Waiting for the sky to take back the rain,
for pale blue and forest green,
tips of twigs shimmer violet and teal,
swift hummingbirds diving beak first
into an aqua pool.
Like the burst of flavour
in a succulent slice of orange,
they call,
Yemaya already sketching
the nectar to blossom.

Pigeon Park

in the nadir of wintry isolation
frosted ash turns the city to stone   eerily quiet
numb   the homeless toss on frigid park benches
traverse solitude
quiet epiphanies in the rhythm of travel
as life catches up with itself
crescent moon evanesces
in the cold sky
reborn each day
into the choice
to continue

shadow girl

i wash my hands till the cracks bleed
and my chipped black nail polish vanishes
the pain we eloquently carry
too deep to be directly spoken   rises
in luring rhythms   glacial rivulets
we bathe it in loquaciousness
make angel wings of heartbreak   abuse   injustice
create feathers   to lift ourselves from it
carving stories through fingertips

the unwanted catch

a crackle of fireworks
fibroids of fishing lines
pull you in
like broken machinery
cinders sink in slow motion
when your hair was in a knot
you separated it strand by strand
to find yourself from underneath
the clutter and anger and dirt of street life
but this is not your mess
and there is nothing of yourself in it

sirens and wind

sirens and wind in the night
the energy of a storm on the way
too hot and too cold all at once
telephone line crosses plastered in white
faith abandoned in a desert of snow

i seek new meaning
write prayers on peace cranes
and float them in the river
a silent procession punctuating the surface
like the salt of my tears on the sheet
in the field of morning ritual

Timeless Soul

How has it been seventeen years,
in some worlds a whole lifetime
of living in BC?
We still call other provinces home,
cities we stayed in only five years,
the place where our paths crossed,
the moment our eyes met,
the winters I waited –
now seventeen seasons pass
in the falling of the cherry petals,
the movement of waves over shore,
the flight of eagles past the window,
frosty nights of stars,
the moon in and out,
a lifetime in a heartbeat.

slender curve of moon
in the cool descending night
yin and yang at rest

Mirage

On a tangerine canvas,
pregnant seahorses
float through the air,
their tails painting the sky,
as I dream in the sun,
looking out on winter
wine and wind.

Your Sweetness Lingers

Flying with you
was the gentlest dream ride,
diamond and alabaster
Stanley Park nights,
Celtic trees and cold air,
your body keeping me warm,
moonlit snowflakes
flickering across the tips of boughs,
your eyelashes caressing my face
in friendship openness,
the spark of your kiss
stirring my desire,
like peppermint tea
tingling through my insides,
rhythmic waves of the sea
enticing us all the way.

Lonely for our conversations,
the frosted pine
on the mountain
wait with me –
i am longing
to laugh with you,
spinning 'round the forest
in your arms,
to love you again
in earth memory.

Softly in Cedar

Moving through the forest
to the place we used to be,
my fingertips brush your ashes,
blending them with memories
you loved,
sensations that touch gently,
yellow rose petals from our garden,
peppermint tea,
drops of moonlit rain,
sounds of the ocean and
spirits of the trees
in the leaves
of your journal,
my love for you.

You Were There

You were there
in lavender sunset swirls
of paint on canvas,
through the grassy terrain
to Sechelt beach,
in the cadence of royal blue shells
the waves washed to shore,
the gentleness you are
finding its way to me,
like the wind breathing cypress
through the grace of long easy days.

You were there
in the tempo of waiting,
the lonely pages
of chapters in time
when I poured
my longing into work,
loving through brokenness.

You were there
in the allegro
of road trips through life,
the toddlers and Labradors and sunflowers
I nurtured as my own
and in the crescendo of mountain trails
leading to Eagle Bluffs.

You are there
outside my bedroom window,
as planes disappear into stars
and the moon fills each night
to watch over and guide and protect
this exquisite gift of existence.

Sleeping with Books

Inhaling the exhilarating
bouquet of new print
by the golden glow
of the reading lamp,
I taste little pieces of prose,
then fall all the way in,
comforted in the texture of pages,
soft as sun-warmed
Belinda's Dream roses,
inviting the inscription of
free verse rhythms
in the sleeve.

Highlighters and ink stars
bleed wild flowers
across aqua-coloured
Egyptian cotton sheets.
Water lilies blossom
in the sapphire satin blanket,
spirals of petals and sepals
arising like northern lights
over Greenland.

Sipping jasmine tea,
in bed with my books,
my soul unto itself,
I speak aloud
my deepest revelations
of passion and awe,
how much I love
the home they are to me.

late autumn sun

now dry desert bone
i breathe in poetry
lie down and remember
royal blue words
serendipity
        falling
like stars

The Zen of Tulips

Like light to the fallen,
late afternoon rays
illuminate the shades
inside lustrous petals,
highlighting a hint of pink
in the leaves
as vivid as tiny translucent shells
from the shore –
sand clings
to the long silky strands of stems,
an earthen reminder
of where we come from
and to which we return.

As I Let Go

amber cradle
moves closer
end of life blessing
half moon
full circle

All These Poems

All these poems
Petals on a purple daisy
Of my life

surrender

I compost my old poems in decomposing fruit
raspberry rivulets
held in the folds of long ago words
      the freedom to move on
drupelets one step ahead
gently into the earth

Wild Flowers

at peace in the finite nature
of this one life
my ashes among wild roses

Poet Profile

Cynthia Sharp is a poet, educator and fiction writer who thrives on interdisciplinary collaboration and peace education. She has been broadcast internationally and published on every continent, if the online *Antartica Journal* counts. She received two honourable mentions in the 2017 Cecilia Lamont Poetry Contest, placed third in The Royal City Literary Arts Poetry Contest in 2015 and was a finalist in The West End Writers poetry contest in 2010. Her work can be found in many literary journals and has been nominated for the *Pushcart Prize* and the *Best of the Net Anthology*.

She is the author of the prose poetry novel *The Light Bearers in the Sand Dollar Graviton* and the editor of *Poetic Portions*, an anthology of poems and recipes honouring Earth Day. She is delighted to be part of the vibrant literary scene in New West and the Greater Vancouver Region. In her spare time, she enjoys walking the sea wall in the exquisite natural beauty of the west coast.